Conversations with the Moonlight

Written by
Jessica Michelle

CONVERSATIONS WITH THE MOONLIGHT
Written & arranged by Jessica Michelle

dedication

I dedicate this to the ones who leave while the tears are still falling. To the souls that are so lost, they have forgotten what "I love you" should feel like. I dedicate this to those who have bled tears in the name of lost love. And to those who have yet to discover what love really is.

Most importantly, I dedicate this to you. You completed my heart when I wasn't trying to fill a void. You gave me the breath to speak when I felt like I might run out of air. I find safety when my head meets your chest. I dedicate this to you Wade, and to the stories we are writing together.

contents

I have silently traveled many roads.
And while there is always so much
to be said, I find myself quiet. Mute.
I lose myself in the words that
should be spoken but never seem
to find a way to escape my lips.
And so, my story remains unheard.
It's nothing more than a conversation
between me
and
the moonlight.

PHASE ONE:
breakdown

I can never seem to find the breath to speak all that you need to hear. Even if I did, I am not sure that you would listen. And so, I write. Our stories remain within these pages and not once do you question my silence.

I am left here to wonder, what do you call a love that isn't love?

night 1

I was drawn to your kiss.
Your lips, magnets.
Pulling me in
every time I was
by your side.
Lost in a trance,
I was completely
intoxicated.
Like a shot of whiskey,
your kiss would burn
my soul.
Bringing me
one step closer to
ecstasy
and two steps
further
from a reality
I so
desperately needed.

I wanted this
to be love.
As hard as I fought
to believe there was
something to us,
I was not naive.
I've always known
I wasn't the first you
let enter your heart.
There were others before me.
I can still see pieces
of their reflections
dancing in your eyes
as you stare back into mine.
And no matter how hard
you try to scrape your soul clean,
they are forever
embedded inside you.
I know that I am not the first
you let enter your heart.
But I pray that I am the last you let
enter into your dreams.

night 4

Your words
made my body
tremble.
With every syllable
that fell from
your lips,
I was thrown deeper into a
world of temptation.
I should know better
than to submit
to your whispers
in the night.
We were playing a
dangerous game.
And I would toss in
all of my chips
to hear you whisper
my name in the dark
one
more
time.

Show me your truth.
All of it.
Every last aching piece.
I need to know
what's pulling me in.
I've seen everything
you share with the world.
But there is more.
Something deeper inside
that keeps bringing me back
to you.
An irresistible force.
A temptation this strong
must be criminal.
And no matter how hard
I try to resist calling for you,
yours is the only name
that falls
from my lips.

night 6

Tonight,
we breathe.
I feel the heat escape
your mouth as you whisper
in my ears.
Your words drip down
my neck
and cover me like
a blanket.
My body was
cold before you.
Freezing
beneath a starless sky.
And now,
together,
we will be the warmth
we have both
been craving.
Even if that's all
we will ever be to
each other.

Every time you feel me
slipping away,
you extend your hand.
Reaching out far enough
for our fingertips
to touch.
You see hope in my eyes and
 pull back.
You never wanted
me this close.
You just didn't want
me far away.

night 8

Tonight,
let's drink.
You will forget
the promises you
whispered in my ear.
And come morning,
I will forget
that for a moment
I believed you.
Either way,
we both win.

night 9

You held me.
Tight.
It was as if you knew it could be the last time
you would feel my ivory skin on
your naked chest.
Yesterday had come and gone,
and you knew that after everything,
tomorrow was no longer a promise I
could make.

You held me.
Tight.
And tonight, despite everything inside of me
saying no, I let you.
I could feel the fear in your fingertips.
They were fighting everything to keep
from holding me any tighter.
You were afraid that this time, I would walk away.
I was afraid I would stay.

You held me.
And tonight, I didn't ask you
to let go.

night 11

We spend our days fighting.
Grasping to hold onto something
that will remind us
of who we used to be together.
The daylight forces us
to remember everything,
shining light on the truth.
But come sunset,
our world changes.
We spend our nights
tangled in smoke stained sheets.
We danced the only way
our souls knew how.
Life was almost forgotten.
We are reminded that
all the empty words
and broken promises
mean nothing
when the lights are
down.

I miss the way our bodies
used to meet in the darkness.
With every night that I feel the moon
smile down on me,
I am reminded of how things used to be.
We would get lost in each other.
Drowning between the sheets.
The only time we would resurface was
to fill our lungs.
You would spend hours tracing the curves
of my body.
Fingertips to skin.
There was no need for words.
We would dance in the
silence of the night.
I didn't know if it was time or fate,
but something was pulling us apart.
Something had changed.
And every time the sun fell from the sky
to kiss the water,
I knew that another day had escaped us.
And we were no closer to where we
used to be.

night 13

I run our story
through my mind
on repeat.
I replay your words
over and over again.
Searching
for an underlying truth.
You play your part quietly.
Chiming in only when I am
about to cross the line.
You get off on my uncertainty.
You have love for me
but you never quite know
what to do with it.
And you would rather have me
search for a story that isn't there,
than admit that you don't know
our ending either.

We used to dance.
Back and forth,
you would make my body sway.
As time passed,
you offered to
take my hand less
and less.
And
in the end, there was
no movement.
We stood there.
Waiting for the other
to make us feel something.
We were forever lost
in the memory
of the music
we used to make.

night 15

A chill makes its way
through our room.
Your body is next to mine.
Our bed is warm,
but the air is cold.
I spend my days
silently thirsting for you.
I bite my tongue.
We can't go there again.
You know the stories
my tears carry.
I don't know if it is
that you are too tired
to keep walking
this road with me,
or if you simply
no longer want to.
But something
has changed,
and I fear that
even though I am
by your side,
I am no longer
in your heart.

I wonder where you've
been all night.
Your body,
of course,
at my side.
But your mind was off
in another world.
Am I with you in your
thoughts?
Or were those
another way to escape me?
I sit here wondering
how long we can keep
this charade going.
Dragging a questionable love
behind us.
Can we keep forcing
something to be
that never really was?
I keep these questions
to myself.
It's obvious,
you have nothing left
to give me now.

night 17

And tomorrow,
when we wake,
our mistakes
won't be forgotten.
Forgiven, maybe.
But we all know
heartache
never really disappears.
We can pretend
that the tears
never happened.
But we live
in a world of lies.
We've been
doing it for years.

I feel us dying down.
Our love, it's almost gone.
I used to fear our intensity.
Never fully giving in.
I would give up just about
anything for one more
night of heat with you.
There are nights,
you would do even more
to get
me to stay away.
I pull.
You push.
But then you call me back.
We are caught up
in an endless game
of tug of war.
I feel myself losing my grip.
The rope is slipping.
And you are sure to
win this round.

night 19

I need more.
Your words are no
longer enough to
get me through the night.
I need you to show me.
To make me *believe*
that all the stories
you are telling my body
are also meant for
my heart.
To give me something
to fight the nightmares that
take over my mind
in the darkest hours.
I need you to grab me.
Just hard enough
to make me feel like
you are the only one who can
take me to the moon
and bring me safely back to earth.
I need to feel you feel me.
But, even at my side,
you are still.

You draw lines
with no intention
of staying within them.
Tie ropes
like you were
the only one
crossing the bridge.
We can go on living,
if we can even call it that.
Forced kisses and empty eyes.
We say we will get through it.
Just a little time until we pass
through this storm.
But we both know the truth.
There is no end in sight.
We will die from exhaustion
or drown from the rain of tears.
Either way, our love is not
getting out of this alive.

night 21

Maybe I am not who
you expected me to be.
My curves don't line up
with the path you have in
front of you.
We have traveled different roads
only to arrive at the same
destination.
And still, we can't seem to agree
where to travel next.
So you can go left.
I will go right.
And if our paths somehow meet
down the road,
then we will know it was meant to be.
Until then, I will hold on to the
hope that someone
out there
is waiting
for me to fill their hand
with mine.

We sit side by side.
Like nothing has changed.
Your skin meets mine.
We both feel it.
There is still a flame.
Hidden beneath the tears
and the walls we've built.
There is still something there.
It may be nothing more
than a mistake,
but tonight,
we risk burning down
to ashes
just to feel something.
Our bodies were meant
to create this fire.
But come morning,
you are gone.
Content with putting out
our flame.
I will never understand how you
can trade it all in
for a life in the dark.

night 24

Playing it safe,
I am careful not to
tip the scales in any
one direction.
I am riding
the line
between madness
and sanity.
So desperately
trying to be
the mirror image
of what I thought
you wanted.
I only wish I had known
that this
was the most
dangerous game
of them all.

Where have you been
all this time?
You run away as quickly
as the wind changes.
Sneaking back just in time
to slip in before you are forgotten.
You tempt my heart
with dreams of tomorrow,
knowing all too well that tomorrow
will never come.
You'll speak about it
as if it is the next step on our
journey together.
But we will never meet it.
You and I are meant for not much more
than this moment.
You've known from the start.
I've tried to sleep through the lies
you've fed me.
But you have found a way to seep
into my dreams.
And I didn't realize until just now,
how hard I had been fighting to keep you here.

night 26

Maybe I am a
little bit of madness.
All of my efforts to keep me
from this have failed
and here I am.
Even though I know that
I am partly to blame,
I will look back on this
with virgin eyes.
Because I know this
is never how I meant
for things to be.
And even in this dark moment,
I would risk it all
just to bring you back.

I'm still holding onto hope.
Like a fool,
I'm waiting for your
love to come back
to me.
I know that someday you
will be just another
memory I drink
to forget.
Just give me a memory
worth holding onto.
Something heavy enough
to weigh down the
moon at night.

night 29

I tell myself that I alone
carry the weight of our past.
That your arms are empty,
bearing none of this load.
I tell myself
that I have taken all of
the hits.
That every sin was thrown
from your hand and meant
solely for my heart.
I ignored the moments you
were quiet
and forgot the lines
I fed you.
Reminding you
of the footsteps
that have led you
away from me.

I wonder why
it took me so long
to realize that not
all love means the
same thing.
We spoke the
same words.
Sang the same
song.
But for some reason,
the four letters that
left my lips
always seemed to
carry more weight
than anything your
mouth could produce.

PHASE TWO:
solitude

I talk myself through each night. I relive every moment and every good bye over and over again. I thought it was you that I missed. But I am beginning to see that it was your warmth that kept me around. And when my bed is empty, I don't miss your touch. I don't miss your hand in mine. I miss thinking that I would always have someone there.

night 1

It's over.
And I am nothing more
than the mess
you have left behind.
Everywhere I look,
there are pieces
of what used to be.
Empty bottles and
broken dreams.
Or is it broken bottles
and empty dreams?
I don't know anymore.
My soul is scattered
in a million pieces.
No matter how hard I try,
I can't seem to pull
myself together.

I'm scared.
This road seems too big
for only one set of
footprints.
The gravel cracks
beneath my feet
and I am so tempted to
turn back.
I know that this path
is right for me.
But movement is scary.
I have been standing
still for so long now,
running free
almost feels
like a sin.

night 6

I didn't know if I had
given up on the idea of
soul mates,
or if I simply lost faith
that I would ever
find mine.
All I know
is that the day
I let go of us
was a sad, sad day
for this
hopelessly romantic
soul.

I put our love on a pedestal.
Making you out to be a God.
As if you were without sin and
unable to hurt me.
I pegged you as someone
I could trust with my soul.
And now, when I step back
and break it down,
maybe nothing was
ever what we made it out to be.
You were never a God.
If anything, you were the devil
dancing on my shoulder.
Tempting me with everything
I could have ever dreamt of.
And in an instant,
stealing it out from underneath me.

night 8

I pretend that there is strength
hidden deep within me.
A strength cultivated from my
own desires.
I pretend that my spine isn't pieced
together by the words you whisper
in my ear at night.
That this passion I feel burning deep
within me, has nothing
to do with the way your hand brushes
my thigh.
I pretend that the intensity
I crave can be satisfied by myself and
myself alone.
I like to pretend, but how will I ever
convince you that I don't need you
if I can't even convince myself?

night 9

There was a time
when you craved my skin.
Naked.
Next to yours.
When my voice was the only song
you played in your mind.
Quiet whispers you would
listen to on repeat.
There was a time when nothing
else mattered as long as it was *my*
body engulfed in *your* arms.
And now, as if we have turned back
the clocks,
your hands are nowhere in sight.
The music has
stopped playing.
And I am once again
alone.

night 11

You sold your soul
for one more shot.
A chaser that you pray
will send me far away
from your dreams.
It's not enough to
make you forget,
just enough to make
you believe
that you no longer care.
Cheers.

I am awake.
Silently speaking all of
the things left unsaid.
These words,
they need to leave me.
But I am not ready
for you
to hear them.
I can't sleep.
Your goodbye is still
echoing through my mind.
And I am kept awake by a voice
that no longer
wants to call my name.

night 14

I should have known
your kiss would
taste of poison.
That the moment
your lips met mine,
your memory,
even after you're gone,
would be burned in my soul
forever.
I would have no hope of
escaping you.
That no matter whose
lips dared to dance
with mine,
the only thing
I would taste
would be the
sweetness you
left behind.

I've been getting by.
Barely surviving.
Shooting whiskey and inhaling
what little bit of your scent is left on
my pillow.
If it were up to me,
I would overdose on your memory.
Grab a handful of soon to be
forgotten stories and swallow them whole.
Letting them take over my body
and send me into a self-induced coma.
My only source of comfort are the
dreams of who we used to be.
But I am stuck here.
Alone.
The whiskey is gone.
I swallow my tears,
hoping to water something new within me.
But there is no hope.
You stole what little life was
still left inside.
I am not sure I will ever recover.

night 19

I fill my glass.
With each sip,
a little piece of you
is cinged from my memory.
I drink to forget the times
you walked away.
Head up
towards the world.
Bearing no shame.
But even more,
I drink to forget the times
that I didn't walk away.
We were once a story
unfolding.
A tale for the generations
to tell.
And now, we are nothing
more than a painful reminder
of late nights stained
with tears
and broken promises.

I sit at the back
of the bar.
Hiding behind my whiskey
and cigarettes.
They shield me from the world.
I shoot whiskey and light up.
The smoke burns my eyes
almost as much as these tears
I've been fighting back.
I don't smoke. It's not for me.
It's nothing more than a distraction.
Something to save me from
having to fake a smile.
I'll sit here.
With empty eyes,
staring at the world we
once shared.
Watching life go on
without me.
Drinking to forget the lies
you have fed me.

night 23

I sleep alone.
There is no movement.
Even the air is still.
No late night sighs of pleasure
to sing me to sleep.
No whispers gently kissing my ear
in the darkness.
You are gone.
And I am left with nothing
but my tears
to keep me company
tonight.

night 24

There is so much more
I want to be,
but I am forever stuck
inside the memory of us.
I try to escape this shadow
you have cast over my heart.
But I am drowning in the
darkness that hovers above me.
You read me your lines as
if straight from a script.
Day after day.
Promise after promise.
I give into the words
you feed me.
And I wonder,
if I were to pile all of your
promises in front of me,
would I sink or swim?

night 26

I can't sleep.
Memories of your head
on my chest flood my mind.
My eyes swell
and I can no longer see the
reality in front of my face.
Maybe it is for the best.
I know that come morning
I will be alright.
All but your scent will be
washed away by my tears.
In the darkness,
I am weak.
But with the morning light,
I can see the truth.

I should have seen it coming.
When you reached
for my thigh
and not my hand.
When your I love you
was whispered only between
my legs and not in my ears.
When you rolled over
as soon as you were finished
with my body.
I should have seen it coming.
My body used to house
your love
but now,
it is only there
to keep you warm at
night.

night 29

You tease my soul.
Walking away
from my arms.
You are still throwing
your love in my face.
Forcing my mind and my heart
to battle to the death.
My brain is begging
me to leave.
But my heart still wants
to believe in you,
holding on to what was.
I try to block you
from my thoughts.
Keep you away.
I'm fighting to keep this war
that is brewing within me
from ever starting.
I already know how our story ends.
By the time you win my heart back,
you will once again be ready to leave.
And I will be left wondering
how I let myself fall for you
all over again.

I admit it.
It's a fault.
Loving the way I do.
When I love,
I love way too hard.
I'm just trying to make
up for the years of you
not knowing how.

PHASE THREE:
lessons

I am at war with myself. I have made promises to keep you away. Signed them with my own tears. And, even though I know you are poison for my soul, I still find your hand falling into mine. I guess some lessons need to be learned more than once.

night 1

I wanted you to hear me.
I needed to let it all out.
To make you understand
just how you made my blood soar.
It raced through my veins.
Damn it. I needed to tell you
just how hard I was fighting
to stay inside my skin.
That when my name leaves your lips,
I feel the weight of
a thousand pounds of bricks
thrown upon my chest.
Crushing my heart,
but sparking life back into me
all at the same time.
I needed you to know
that I am lost.
A part of you still has a hold on me.
But, that I loved you more than anything
at the same time.
I had so many words for you.
But when I looked in your eyes, I lost my voice.

night 4

We stopped and stared.
Searching for the words to say.
As if they would fix the ones
already spoken.
Your fingers fumbled across
my lips the way they have
a million times before.
Desperately wanting to pull
the answers from my tongue.
But there was nothing
to be said.
You looked in my eyes
and I turned away.
I couldn't face our truth.
Not yet.
You grabbed my hand
and just as quickly
let it go.
In one breath,
we knew it was goodbye.

night 7

It's like every word that I want to say
has already been spoken.
There is nothing new for me
to spit into the world.
Nothing that will catch your attention.
And every time I try to tell you how I feel,
you stare at me blankly.
Because all you see are tears.
All you hear is white noise.
In a way, you find this comforting.
Background noise that you secretly
pray never fully disappears.
Part of you wants me around,
in the shadows of your world.
You want me there in the dark
with you.
But you can't fully commit.
You are not ready to turn
me off completely.
You slowly tune me out.
Hoping that eventually you will
forget that it was my noise that
used to send you to sleep.

Maybe the safest place for my love
wasn't within your arms.
I am slowly beginning to feel
your fingers lace around my neck.
Ready and willing to choke the
life out of my soul.
Tightening your grip
a little more each day.
You lie to me.
Telling me that you are here
to help me find my way.
But just as I take my last breath,
I realize that this was your way
of surviving.
You couldn't live in a world
in which I was so willing
to breathe on my own.

night 10

It's taking everything in me
not to scream out for you.
But even if your name
manages to leave my lips,
they won't leave in a
cry of passion.
I won't be begging you to stay.
I would be cursing you
to Gods I don't even believe in.
Begging them to rain down on you
the same ugliness you have
inflicted on my soul.
You are not
the man you claim to be.
You dress the part.
But now,
even your threads are starting
to wear thin.
And I can suddenly see through
everything you are so desperately
trying to hide behind.

I drank.
But this time, it wasn't to forget.
I wanted to remember.
I needed to let the pain burn
deep in my soul.
Every time I brought the bottle
to my lips, I would pray,
"Lord, let this be it."
I needed this to be the sip that
pushed me over the edge.
The sip that kept me from forgetting
the sound of your footsteps walking away.
I never want to forget the emptiness
you left me with.
I needed my tears to pump
through every vein in my body.
I couldn't risk forgetting
and letting you back
into my heart.

night 13

Some letters
are not meant to be sent.
These words, to you,
are not worth the postage.
So I will keep them to myself.
Each word spilled onto the paper
from my heart,
a trophy of what once was.
And just like all the others,
soon these words will line the
bottom of the waste bin.
Worth nothing more than
its weight in the world.

I have been
fighting this battle
for so long
I have forgotten
what the war was about.
It's not so much
that I am afraid
to lose.
I just know
that I don't want
you to win.

night 15

I am choking on words I've yet to say.
I should have fed them to you long ago.
But I sit here. Quietly.
The words run through my mind.
I could force feed them to you.
Make you gag as I shove them into
your consciousness.
I've had to keep them down for
so long.
They eat away at my being.
And just when I think its
time for you to digest
what I have been tasting,
I stop.
I know all too well
that you would never survive
half of what I have.

night 16

I am walking away.
Every step forward is one
step further from you.
One foot in front of the other.
Even though that is about
all I can muster right now,
I am certain that come nightfall
you will be nowhere in sight.
I know it won't be enough.
When I see the moon
standing alone in the empty sky,
I will find myself missing your arms.
And I will be thrust back into a
state of uncertainty.
Wondering not only how I got here,
but how the hell will I ever
find my way back.

night 18

Grasping for straws,
I've been holding on
for too long.
I feel you slipping
through my fingers.
But it's not you that
I am letting go of.
You aren't you.
You've changed direction
and forgot to invite me
along for the ride.
It's not *you* that I am letting go of.
I am letting go of the you
I always hoped you would
once again become.

There was a time I would
travel the world for you.
All day.
All night.
Down crooked streets.
Through empty towns.
There was a time
when the thought of you
was enough to get me through
a sleepless night on the road.
A time when you were worth it all.
It is funny how quickly things change.

night 23

If it's your all or nothing,
let it be nothing.
Your all has left me with
broken promises
and empty memories.
There may be scattered pieces
of happiness lost somewhere
in the rubble.
But the dangers of digging them up
far outweigh the rewards.
So our love will stay buried.
It seems this is the only
way our hearts will come out
of this whole.

I am beginning to see
that this is
nothing more than a game.
Back and forth.
Like a coin toss,
you are hoping to
land heads up.
I flip you as many times
as you flip me.
There was no winner in
this game of love.
Just a couple of bruised egos
and some pocket change.

night 26

And if your kisses
were as sinful
as your intentions,
well,
that would be
a different story.
You leaving me
breathless
instead of tear stained,
that might be
something
worth sticking
around for.

I would rather
choke
on a mouthful of
flowers
than live
with a handful of your
promises.
Both will eventually lead
to my demise.
But, at least with the flowers,
I will have a little
beauty to take
with me to the grave.

night 28

I've killed our love with
expectations.
Murdered
in broad daylight
by everything I was waiting
for you to be for me.
I don't feel remorse.
But I do mourn the loss.
I don't know if these expectations
were created solely by me
or if you helped me dream
them up.
Either way,
our love is dead.
And I see no hope of
revival.

You walked away.
I knew it would be
the last time
I could watch you leave.
This time, things would be
different.
There would be no chasing you.
There would be no tears.
The only thing left to do was drink.
And so,
I drank.
But not for you.
For your taste.
Doing everything I could
to wash the taste of
your lies
away.

night 30

I gave myself a minute.
Just one to mourn what
has been lost.
To remember the way you
curled your lip when you
said my name.
To remember the way your
aftershave clung to
my chest
after we had become one
under the sheets.
I gave myself a moment
to grieve everything that
I was so ready to lose.
I know that I have a lifetime
ahead of me full of
moments without you
dancing in my mind.
But this moment,
right now,
this is for you.

PHASE FOUR:
awakening

I am finding myself in a world that doesn't carry your scent. I can breathe on my own. And for the first time in so long, I can sleep without you lingering in my dreams.

night 1

Soon you will be just
another memory I regret.
A love letter thrown
to the flame.
An old Polaroid
torn in two.
You will linger
in the back of my mind.
When I think of you,
I will smile.
Not because of the memories
that we share.
But because I finally realized
that I survived you
without ever knowing it.

Temptation won the battle
within me today.
I gave in.
There was no fight.
No blood.
There were no tears
passed from my eyes to yours.
I've been watching you
push forward.
Half-assed
and full grinned.
And I finally decided,
that I too
no longer care
about this war.

night 4

I am a mess.
Staging riots in my own
heart just to feel something.
I don't know what I want.
But I sure as hell know what
I don't.
I spend my days fighting
with my demons.
But come night, I remember
the beauty they bring to me
and together we dance.
I am a mess.
And for the first time,
I found someone to love me
for it.
Me.

Not knowing
if I am coming
or going
is proving to be
one of the most
exhausting moves
of my life.
I haven't
even taken my first
step yet.
I can no longer
stand still.
It is time to
let go of everything
I knew to be true.
Freeing up room
in my heart
for what is to come.

night 8

Learning to accept
this twisted
and never ending
road that I am on.
The scenery keeps changing,
but I can't seem to shake
this feeling of deja vu'.
Maybe one day
I will realize that
all of these detours
are mile markers
on the path
that will someday
lead me
down the road
I am meant to travel.

I am more than
the broken pieces of memories
scattered on the floor.
More than
your footsteps walking away
from my heart.
I am more than
the tears that fled my eyes
at midnight.
I am the soul
that replayed those memories
in the darkest of times.
I am the eyes
that saw past the ugliness
in the world.
I am built
from the dreams
I carry with me.
I am a
heart completely free.

night 13

You never seem to
understand my intentions.
Determined to see only the
darkest possibility when there was light
right in front of you.
You always assume that I was here to
capture every last breath
you hold inside.
That I wanted all of you.
And, despite my efforts
to make you hear the truth,
you refuse to take me at
my word.
Never understanding what a
burden it would be
to carry all that you are.
I never wished to hold
all of you.
I just wanted to keep close
the pieces of you that saw beauty
in me when I couldn't.
But now, that is a weight
I no longer wish to carry.

I was always so willing
to give up pieces of myself
to make you feel whole.
Never realizing that I was
silently breaking down what little
of me was still standing strong.
I can no longer survive on your
broken promises
and half truths.
Your strong hands and firm grip
do nothing but warm my bed at night.
I need you for more than just
the comfort in the darkness.
If there isn't enough of you
left to give me,
then all I have to offer you
are these footsteps
as I walk away.

night 15

Surviving us
was my only
option.
Forget what I wanted.
To move on,
I would need to
recover from this
disease once known as
our love.
It was infected.
Boils of ugliness surfacing.
I searched for a cure.
Something that would breathe
life back into this decaying
marriage of our two hearts.
But we both know,
there is no antidote known
to man that could cure a
disease as cancerous as
your love.

You say that I am broken and bruised.
That you can see my scars from a mile away.
I try to blame you.
Your arms promised me paradise.
It turns out, you are nothing more
than an oasis.
And I am weathered and worn
from the days spent thirsting for
your love.
But I know I will come out of this
stronger than ever.
I thirst and thrive for so much
more than you have ever tossed my way.
For now, I live in darkness.
But I can see light off in the distance.
I know that soon these scars will
heal and you will no longer recognize me.
The girl you knew carried the weight of
your words on her shoulders.
And soon, I will be free of everything
you once used to hold me down.

night 19

I turn my head
and claim that I carry no fear.
This weight on my shoulders
is nothing more
than shadows
dancing on my back.
It has nothing to do with your
footsteps walking away.
They have traced every vein
pumping life into this
dying heart.
I claim I carry no fear,
because you no longer carry
any weight in my heart.
Both are lies I tell myself
so that maybe I can dream
without tears
for one more
night.

I dried my eyes
and realized
that my soul
no longer mourned
the loss of your touch.
I used my tears
to water
something *new*.
Something *strong*.
Something *beautiful*.
It was a new beginning that
I would never let you
be a part of.
Tonight,
this was *enough*
to keep me going.

night 23

I let myself burn.
Deep within my bones.
Nothing remains but ashes.
I am waiting for the smoke to settle.
And once the skies clear,
I will emerge from the
smoldering rubble.
Reborn.
Free of the chains I once
bound myself with.
A sinful distraction to pass the time.
Now I am naked.
Basking in my truth.
All that's left of the past are
my stories.
Words I once whispered with
hopes that someone would hear me
now fill the air.
Echoing.
I was lost for so long in a world
promising me love.
I am leaving it behind to discover
the fire that is igniting within me.

We have fallen apart.
Pieces of what we were
are crumbling to the ground.
I am buried beneath these
shattered memories and
twisted intentions.
They are crushing me.
I try to dig my way out.
But no matter how hard
I try to remove the rubble
you have left behind,
I can't seem to escape you
completely.
I am left with no choice
but to embrace
these shards of what
once was
and rearrange
all of the brokenness
until something beautiful
breaks through.

night 27

It wasn't that I was
slipping away.
I was letting go.
And in a way, this was
far more painful.
It was a choice.
I was slowly releasing my grip
on the past.
Hoping to make room
for the new love that
I was desperately seeking.
I was short of breath.
Suffocating
in a world that was so new,
but oddly familiar.
I've been here before.
But like a fool
I was so sure
I would never return.
Fate is known for playing malicious
tricks on our hearts.
Creating chaos and turmoil
right when
our waters start to calm.

And now,
I could feel myself
being pulled
under by the waves.
For a moment,
I let myself
slip beneath the surface.
Taking water on the way I
 had taken *you* on;
quiet on the outside,
but screaming within.
I know that if I stay below the water,
 all of my pain
will be washed away
and you would be forgotten.
But I would be left without
the hope of swimming back
to the shore.
I just wasn't sure
if forgetting you was
worth missing the sunrise.

night 30

I stood there.
Waiting for proof
that I could survive.
Proof that I would resurface from this
hole I had buried myself in.
I was waiting for a sign
from the Heavens
that I would find
the strength to get
through this hell.
And through all the time
I spent waiting,
I made it.

PHASE FIVE:
discovery

I have found strength in the silence of the night. The darkness used to fill me with fear. It covered me in a blanket of loneliness. But now I have you next to me. You found me when I wasn't looking to be found. I hid myself from the ugliness of the world. But you, you have shown me that beauty can still be found in the darkness.

night 1

Seduce me
with your words.
I have felt
hands like yours
before.
But that mouth,
I know
those lips
can speak to me
like no one else has.
Spell your love
out for me,
one syllable at
a time.

night 2

It wasn't about what you gave me,
but what you took from me.
You took
the quiet moments that
left my mind to wander alone,
and filled the silence
with whispers of love.
You took away
the cold that was keeping
me from sleeping at night,
and filled not just my bed
but my soul with a fire that
has yet to burn out.
You took the loneliness
that was weighing down on
my shoulders,
and helped me to breath once more.
You took the memory
of a broken heart that has
been dwelling inside me for so long,
and filled it up with love.
You have taken so much more
than you have ever given.
And, for that, I love you.

night 3

Scattered bottles.
Cigarette holes in our sheets.
You.
Next to me.
Last night.
I am begging my mind to
let me remember
the madness of it all.
Our bodies met
in perfection.
Fitting together
like the last
two pieces of a puzzle.
We drank until we spun.
And then danced to
bring us back to earth.
It wasn't our first
midnight dance.
It sure as hell
wouldn't be our last.

night 4

Your hands traveled
 my body.
Your fingers
danced across my chest.
Taking their time to consume
every last inch of me.
Your hands never left me.
Pausing only for a brief moment,
to inhale your cigarette.
You pulled me in closer.
We exhaled.
Tick tock.
Tick tock.

night 5

I was safe.
As soon as your arms
wrapped around my body,
I knew it.
I was safe.
No matter how ugly the stories
swimming in my head were.
No matter how tempting it
was to believe the fears
taking over my heart,
I was safe.
Your arms brought
the only truth my soul
needed.

You pushed
the hair away from my eyes.
Letting your fingers
dance slowly
across my face.
You told me
I was beautiful.
I was everything you
never knew you needed.
You asked
how I had been able
to slip through the fingers of those
before you.
I was the spark
you needed
to keep your soul alive.
And you swore
to me you would
do anything to keep
this fire going.

night 7

I wasn't looking
for answers in the way
your lips parted
when you spoke to me.
I was looking
for answers in the words
your body sang
when the music began
to play.
When there was nothing
between
our two naked souls
but the love we share.
I was looking
for answers in the way
your fingers spoke my name.
Loud enough for only
my soul to hear.

You never kept me
guessing.
With every second
that passed,
and with every
breath that escaped
your mouth,
you made sure I
knew that *mine*
was the soul *your*
body craved
in the darkest hours
of the night.
You were different
than the others.
You knew
that if you didn't convince me
of your hunger;
of yearning for me,
someone else surely would.
And my heart
was not something
that you wanted
up for grabs.

night 9

I want you
to take me.
Not as if I am
your first,
but the last love
you will ever consume.
Sample me
like I am the
sweetest nectar,
Take your time
so as not to
devour all of me
in one gulp,
Savor
every
last moment
that I am by your side.
When it's time
for you to leave,
remember what I am
made of,
and always
come back
for seconds.

night 10

You touched me.

Made me feel alive.

Your hand on my shoulder,

your fingers gently

kissing mine.

Your skin had a cosmic effect on me.

When our naked frames met,

I melted.

My body gave into yours.

Every movement.

Every shift.

We became one.

night 11

Dream about me.
If there is any hope for our
love to survive in this ugly world,
I need you to dream about me.
And not just when you are asleep.
Dream of me
when your eyes are heavy
but the day is still young.
Dream of me
when your voice is weak
but you still have so much
to say.
Dream of me
when you are too angry
to speak my name.
We could lose
ourselves to this
world at any minute.
Promise to dream of me,
even when I am no where
in sight.

night 13

My head
dropped from
your shoulders.
Finally
finding a home
on your chest.
Nestled between
the cage that houses
your heart.
I can hear your
soul calling my name.
I am finally
ready to answer.

night 14

Your words were like
fingertips tracing the
curve of my lips.
Every time
you took a breath,
I stopped breathing.
Waiting for the poetry
to spill from your mouth.
I could feel myself falling
deeper and deeper
into your spell.
I was mesmerized.
Lost in a trance
I hope I never
escape.

night 16

I find peace
in your presence.
Every night I thank
God for your arms.
Not just for the
way they wrap around me
and warm my soul.
Not just for the way you
grab me and pull
me in close.
But for everything you take on.
For the weight you
can bear.
You are the first man
I can trust to
carry my nightmares
away.

night 18

Dip me
in your ink.
Cover me with
words
so powerful
that your body
can no longer
contain them.
Forget silence.
My body
is your canvas.
Paint your love
on me.

I wasn't lost.
I wasn't looking
for my way.
I was solid.
Stable.
At least that is
what I was telling
myself.
I was straddling the line
of sanity
and madness.
Until I found you.
You were my anchor.
You never pulled
me under,
just kept my
mind from drifting
away from
the shore.

night 20

When you dream
of us,
dream of both
sweetness and tears.
Please don't ever
let your dreams
be better
than our
reality.

night 22

Without ever speaking
a word,
your mouth told me stories
that left me hungry
and craving seconds.
And by god,
I would listen to the
stories spilling from
your lips
all night.

night 24

I want your breath
on my breath.
Your lips
on mine.
Seized in a endless
embrace.
I want to bottle
this heat;
this ecstasy.
I want to
be able to taste
this moment
forever.
Never waking
from this
dream.

We laid together.
All night.
Your arms wrapped
around me.
A shield from the
dangers of the night.
I was haunted by my dreams.
Memories brought back
to life while I slept.
You knew you couldn't
fight my demons.
But you could always
be there for me
when I woke up.

night 27

You craved more
than my body
you were after
my words.
To you,
they were music.
You would string them
together.
Writing the most
enchanting lullaby.
They were the only
thing that could
soothe your
lost soul.

Your fingers know
every curve
of my body.
Every dimple.
Every inch.
Your love protects me.
Keeps me safe at night.
I love the way you touch me.
But even more,
I love
how you love
to touch me.

night 30

There is more to this conversation
than the sum of our two naked bodies
under the moonlight.
I listen to the words
your skin whispers to me.
Meant for only
my heart to hear.
Your fingertips,
they beg me to stay.
My mind,
in your eyes, off in another world.
You pull away
and wonder
how it is that I could leave you.
But what you don't seem to understand
is that I take you with me
everywhere I go.
I carry your whispers.
They are rooted within the pockets of my soul.
And just when I think all hope is lost,
I dig deep and find that
you are still with me.
are still with me.

It is a beautiful thing to have you listen to the words as they fall from my lips. The moonlight always understood why I loved the darkness. But you, my love, have made me crave the sunrise. Because only then, can I see your eyes staring back into mine.

Dear you,
There are some words that
are never meant to be spoken.
And, eventually, you will get
to the point where your heart
can no longer contain them.
The tears will come either way.
Spill your heart onto
these pages and let your soul
begin to heal.

xoxo always,
jessica michelle

just me

I am a woman struggling to rediscover my voice after hiding it for far too many years. Some days the words flow from my fingers, and some days, my pages sit dry and empty. I am a mother and a lover. I live off of cold espresso drinks. I am a hopeless romantic and will always be a believer that love will save us all, but only if we let it.

Find me -

Website - jessicamichelle.bigcartel.com/

*Instagam - @_jessica.michelle_*

Facebook - https://www.facebook.com/SimplyJessicaMichelle/

Email - JessicaMichelle.poet@gmail.com

so much love for

Alison Malee, your support through this project has been invaluable. Your love and guidance is more appreciated than you will ever know. Thank you for everything.

My Words With Queens sisters, the miles and hours that may seperate us have not kept me from being able to call you family. Thank you for your support and love. I adore you all.

77557387R00086

Made in the USA
Middletown, DE
23 June 2018